Michelle Whittaker

SURGE

D0875143

great
weather
for MEDIA

Surge
© Michelle Whittaker 2017

Printed in the United States of America

First Edition
ISBN: 978-0-9981440-1-6
Library of Congress Control Number: 2017941669

Cover painting: "Resonance 1" by Dawn Lee (www.dawnleeart.com)
Author photograph: June Whittaker
Book design: Jane Ormerod

Editors: Jane Ormerod, Thomas Fucaloro, David Lawton,
Aimee Herman, Mary McLaughlin Slechta

great weather for MEDIA, LLC
New York, NY

www.greatweatherformedia.com

In Memory of Kurt

For Mom & Dad

Contents

I. In the Afterlife

II. Surge of Light

III.   In the Afterlife of Children

SURGE

Everyone who is born holds dual citizenship, in the kingdom of the well and in the kingdom of the sick. Although we all prefer to use only the good passport, sooner or later each of us is obliged, at least for a spell, to identify ourselves as citizens of that other place.

—Susan Sontag, *Illnesss as Metaphor*

I.

In the Afterlife

A Partial Cento of Visible Light

When we met in secret beyond
swamp and scrubland

"Marriage has teeth," the priest said
tentative, but you and I are seasoned

lovers, khaki rifles, and uniforms
within the walls' white profusions.

I see you wait, as I have, for an angel
we hadn't like to begin with to emerge

with hammers and ladders—
Do you remember my brother's wedding?

I could have done a Joan of Arc,
as the last breath lodged in a man's throat

if I had left for Venezuela with you—
but after too many bottles of white rum

I knew you were on a moving boat
learning how to lose yourself,

and it would be discussed for weeks after,
as if you were the young man with a nail in his foot

like a shell marked souvenir on the shelf.
Don't quote me, but this is all:

Here I am now, without you, looking around
the bedroom with its mix of sex and sleep:

a white tricycle missing both pedals
nestles in me for no apparent reason—

dead-white, wax-white, cold—
head tilted over the board,

like a reverence for the law of gravity
and having owned it for so long

is a daughter, without children,
seeing the light, forming, seeing—

A Bishop in the Sky

after Elizabeth Bishop

A storm hunts the firmament.
I think how they must look now:

Paumanok's forked-tail lying out,
unimpressed by the lightning

in light, like a pair of taciturn twins.
As the storm hunts for an outskirt

I think of Montauk and the lighthouse
as a young couple in separate beds.

I think hail, she, otter, he, shale, him, mussel, her
all wrecked from a nexus of bourbon-scotch

as the artery of sails turn inside the harbor.
The storm hunts the upstairs, and for what—

not for a fiery mangrove view or motorized
above a brawny boat, but rather behind

the easel by the window, pouring a black tea
into a cup of sugary. I think how they must look:

the naked, set to cause a disturbance.

After Dinner

The man is waiting to be unzipped,
is a line I'd say not into writing.

Perhaps the old man is waiting to zip,
is a line from a poem I would also not write.

Inside the old man's mustache, she is one sheep-eyed finger.
I would say she's fool pulling inside his beard hide.

I would write, here gathers grenadier stillness,
the blushed lips suckle on more than milky

as the man looks wise at his cupping hands.
It is here she learns how she's instrumental.

After the Funeral

inside the cordgrass
follow the trails
of snow and pale-blue eggs
of dark-eyed Juncos

inside the cordgrass
the stratus of dusk
hovers mollusks siltstone
and what's left of a kayak
skeletal with one paddle

inside the cordgrass
near a vacant blanket
a sandpiper's black hole
of a flank lays covered
in nest mites

inside the cordgrass
a small horseshoe crab
upturned and overstretched
between a small blue deckchair
rests greener than the seaweed

inside the cordgrass
lounge two sand tombs
small for a hermit crab
and prayer card

inside the cordgrass
hoar frost and skins burn
above the name *Nana* once
stick drawn inside a heart shap

inside the cordgrass
a slender discharge
of breath enters a slender
snow squall inside the course

grasses inside the coarse grasses
mouths and limbs keep tent
as a fragile piston stutters
into parts of what's darkening

Hunt

you think I am lovely hunt,
but there is a no in my moan,
there is wanted rest from my soothsaying
my oh my trailing thigh off in your mouth.

Five Transient Months

i.

The sea hands its body
to the wind.
The wind hands its body
to the sand.
The sand orbits.

ii.

Down shore
children cancel
each other's words.
Their voices tourist
along the coast.

iii.

At the crest, a little girl
breaks away with a tubular
sac shaped float.
She enters as if she's amniotic,
shaking the years clean.

iv.

During dehydration:
I held no name, but
there was a barking dog,
a puncture, a howl drawn,
a thrust, a clot,
an impasse.

v.

During the dream:
A streetlight flickers.
Four men pass me.
They are English, bloody tired.
In an alley,
children stone each other
killing time.
I need to tell you
that I miscarried.
I can't find your street.

On a car, an alarm and I wait.

The Madrigal Body

The last "o" in *morto*
sacred in whole beats
almost strongholds
a sonogram seated
below the copious ribs
of the southwest
corner of a barely-
breasted torso.

I often think of
the masked intruder
who knifed this home
who broke the hinges
who stole the jewels.

Ars Poetica

These exoskeletons
named remipedes
seem humble to me,
but they are rare
dissolvers of oxygen,
bounded as sediments.
They are minikin
orphans, beseechers
swelling their thorax
onto conical mounds.
Their fangs grapple
for mostly brine shrimp,
but hiders they are—
not scarfskin, not leather,
but transparent in a sub-
aqueous dark closet—and free.
What luck, they can freely
be themselves: paragons,
Jurassic, poison-happy,
and timed to be tightly
blind—although they can see,
maybe that's how the silence sees
beneath the current.

Zen Press to Ithaca

push your feet
together
into a stretch
and let us pray
with an open eye
like a peephole
let the mouth pucker
each other we suck
today butterscotch
tomorrow tootsie
and yet there will be
no rolling around
no tasty
no chew on this
no fun
the hip of her
and yet no fat
the hip of him
and yet no guts
there will be
no hairy situations
for we are like a sea
making space
with a stone-size hole
for calypso and canoe
as we pray
on empty
with emptier

let us
be our own lungs
with the sages
letting go
as anchors apart

Stones formerly known as Love

it is passing
       like stones through a window,
            knuckles through a glass door,
                 irises through light,
   shifts from a stare
      like bedsprings from beating,
a spread passes bread on a table,
         as a cocktail stirs untouched.
              a gold ring passes through my legs
           as a teacher passes out a test.
a love story passes through you,
                several times in fact,
           as I watch the passing driver run on through a Stop

In the Afterlife

What comes to mind is Kurt.
He's the first thought rather than lost,
and I imagine his mother godmothering
at his grave, reimagining his austere earth
closed, and then what comes to mind spasms
like the cramp of a charley horse tasking for the heart
and go ahead, call me deficient, like the canary
I watched hit its yellow off a barn window
when in fact what comes to mind is a German, like a shepherd
groaning at acres of birds, or for another bone to pick
or carrot to snap as we wallow in the nude,
as ginger wades in disease, as Echinacea wades in the brain
and while boiled rice misgoverns as overcast
rosin waits as a diamond at the knuckle
but really, what comes to mind
is dehydrated, an apricot warping in his mouth
as we sit inside a waterfall's cave, go on past
Walnut Creek around the Zion Zoar Zion Valley
if I could only remember
the feel of his broad shoulder, like an empty ball-court
against my shoulder as he grabs for the broken spine of Siddhartha

but we don't really need to talk about that fact
and we don't really need to talk about the thunder
thundering inside the house
where he died:

but if only I'd formed the letters into the words of a letter
a day sooner a day sooner than the brain understood a day sooner
his heart unharnessed into the glory of heat like any first love asking
any first lover for more time one more time like any want in the glory
of need to remove the gladiolus from its head into a stainless pot to
boil then steep into he who is the risen the risen heat

Blank Canvas

My favorite frigid
black ring of a crow
now sits soluble.

The green lovers
and the green timberline
have all gone to mud.

The two orange monks
under the honey locusts
have stopped wavering.

Where he unclothed
aside Cayuga Lake
is now an obligatory fog.

The more I search for him
the more distant
I recall a red cabin door left.

What we look like:

The Engagement Ring

and so off you went
      sliding off the fourth;
            sliding off the make me weak one
the one who makes
      a child cry and drill again
            on a piano key
while Listen, to them
      blue jays fight
            from the outside. Listen
how they tribe
      note after no
            after no

WARNING REPORT

SURGE: IMPACT UNFOLDS
ACROSS COASTAL AREAS
OF LONG ISLAND.
INUNDATION LOCALIZES
WITH A STORM SURGE:
FLOODS BEYOND
IMMEDIATE SHORELINES,
AND FARTHER INLAND—
HIGHER WATER
OVERSPREADS ONTO
ROADS AND PARKING LOTS
AS CONDITIONS DANGEROUS—
SURGE: WATER ROAMS
THE ROADWAYS, AS BEACH ERODES
HEAVY SURF BREACHES THE DUNES,
AND WITH INDIFFERENCE—
SURGE: IMPACTS AS IF HUMAN
USUALLY VULNERABLE
BUT STRONG AND FREQUENT
RIPPING LIKE CURRENTS BREAKING
THOSE FROM THEIR DOCKS,
MARINAS, AND MOORINGS.
SURGE: HYPER WATER AND WIND
CONTINUE CROSSING
MID-EASTERN LONG ISLAND—
VOCALIZES WITH HAIL—
DAMAGE CONCERNS
DO NOT INVOLVE OTHER SPECIES,

EXCEPT FOR PETS AND FARM
PRODUCTS, ROOFS, AND SIDING
ALONG WITH PORCHES,
CARPORTS, AND SHEDS.
POWER TOOLS, GENERATORS, GAS LINES
AND BUILDINGS ARE EXPERIENCING
FAILURES IN THEIR FRAMEWORK
LIKE BONE FRACTURES AND BLOCKAGES
LIKE PORTENT ANTENNAS ON
MOBILE AND IMMOBILE HOMES
MILES AWAY UNANCHORED, UNSECURE
THAT MIGHT BECOME DANGEROUS
PROJECTILES, LIKE TREES
SNAPPED OR UPROOTED,
LIKE SIGNS BLOWN INTO
IMPASSABLE LARGE DEBRIS,
SURGE WARNING: WARNING
FOR HUMANS AND HABITATS
SURGE WARNING: IMPACTFUL
DECISIONS: DECISIONS: DIVISIBLE
PLACES AND PLACEMENT
SHOULD YOU STAY OR CONTINUE
TO CROSS BRIDGES, CAUSEWAYS,
AND ACCESS ROUTES—
SURGE: WHAT WILL WE BECOME
PRETENDING WE ARE AS DURABLE
AS THE MANMADE POWERLINES
PLACED AS STRAINED TENDONS
BENEATH THE LOOSENING SPOILS

Flat Winds also known as Tornado

seeing you maneuver
as ill-paced as my grandmother's gait—
meandering the house across the way—
it's like you need be getting into everybody's
business, sweeping up, editing the gardenias,
breaking what's not gopher wooden and concrete
until soft against your arms, like a worrisome
relationship between sickness and recovery—

but some say when it comes to catharsis and lust
you just got to keep busy,
some might say you got your own set of rules,
some even say you've earned sanctimonious,
but most are scared plains of your power,
calling wisdom an avoidance—
almost like those who might pray with you
even if they don't believe to understand
when in great darkness there is the light
of sirens ringing off like chimes belling away

After the Emergency

after Matthea Harvey

While no one operates,
she gives me a facemask, minutes
splinter, seconds schism—she emits
vexation to hands which discover

three degrees of elbowroom, as
sighing seems to quiet the lightning
for slits that break down the dermal.

Let the hand feel the flat-broke
heart, says the Buddhist.

So—this is the afterlife, doctored.

Finite.

The Composer's Reunion

Like in the language of an open window:
the colleague said he dislikes the shrimp, and she agreed,
she dislikes the onkus of its blue vein staring off as a contrapuntal lifeline.

A Mirror of Deflection

Inside the Pyrenees
on the Camino
the way of Santiago
I dreamt of coins
thrown at the feet
of a phone operator
clothed like clergyman
in full-bodied amice
alb and cincture
I dreamt a warning
about the oncoming
rain in his voice
I thought it might rain
enough to create another
breed of beast for I realized
I was neither man nor womb
but like a fulmar shot down
off an olive tree
into a mythical sea
Inside the sea
squid and whale
ate around the bullet
until water was water
and I & I
scalloped the shore
like into pilgrims
where I returned
inside the invisible

search for your voice
Inside the murmurings
where we were indivisible
emanations
where we were
emanations enough
to be a polar front
and if needed
torrential

II.

Surge of Light

Surge

I'm not Your work.
I'm not Your circumference
rimmed honeyed Artois turned upside as glass
treated oddly as an end.

You are the conundrum,
the rummy derelict eel fascinated with genitalia, as I am—
but we are not roommates here, lounging our moods

and I'm not Your work.
I'm not Your broken entertainment used
as a quick fix for a revision.

We are not grammar beginning green, are we?
We are not really authors in exchange—

Trust me,
I wish I could acupuncture Your sabbatical.

A Mirror of a mirror

i.

The legacy:
was advice
to have two children
to keep around the house
like two Bibles
in case one goes missing.

ii.

I used to take red crayon
and scribble on homemade nail polish
and my   would find out
and take that raw sienna belt
that whip, whip, whip
spoke with a witty rip
and by nightfall my hands
blossomed into numb and dumb.

iii.

Actually, on staring at my fingers for a good five minutes,
they look like the legs of a muddy elephant.

iv.

It was such a shock
to be told I am a kinda coffee mark
that accidently sat her fat self
on perfect cleanliness.

v.

At sunset
me and the boy
walked south
on the sod farm
behind the house
and took an orange blanket
from the trunk, and wrapped ourselves
as Buddhist monks,
and found a spot of life for us to lie about.

vi.

You know, a brother and a sister
are not child's play you can stitch on a happy.

vii.

The memory of my   is like
watching an anxious pup hide tidbits
of milk bones round and round he goes
around the house.

viii.

I am suspicious of any kiss that hisses,
and there ain't no Jesus here.
Any spatula-face who rises from the couch
of this house, I move as a mouse.

ix.

I think to be nine.
I think to be ten.
I think to be an age

when I show
my sharp teeth too.

   x.

Even inside the corner pantry, he found me
purpling like a radish, you know, the red one
with the bright white in the middle
once you cut it all up.

   xi.

How strange my torn fibers
how he stares and stomps
my voice, labored under a table
thinking to our God—
it is so unlovely to be unlovely

   xii.

I remind myself
an old man and a young man
is like an old   and a young
the old man is the young man
I remind myself
the young   is the old
which reminds myself
the old daughter is the young daughter
I remind myself
    forced solicitation taught her this.
           taught her how to lay and lie.

Even when I'm the image of
a homeless hitchhiker watching
silently for violence within
humans self-reflecting
into their knives at mealtime,
I'm still not Your work.

***

When dark doors
move slow in the night
I know this ain't Christmas.

A Mirror of the Black Swallowtail

I wish you were the father
of my early years: forever
a cocoon. I wish you were
not the full-winged black
console in the kitchen
demanding the water
pressure be a lesser but
perfected pressure from
a single-handed faucet.
I wish I could see selves
not as deflectors of dirty
dishwater, or as imaging discs
disturbed during the spell
of incubation. Every time
I catch sight of your eyes
the language of knives
sink to skin, sharpening faces.
I wished the silk screen
divided our antennas, legs,
and genitalia. I wished
we never touched.
I wished for the workings
of prayer on species that look a lot
like fallen angels restraining their flesh
under the splayed shadow of negligence.
I wish us back to our Maker
pressured perfectly to reform
on what it means to be
human and conditioned.

I am not Your work
even when I was left
in the corner alone
with the garage boys,
the mirages of men,
the broken whims—

even when he left me
with the ones who played Hell,
You left me
with the ones who played Hell,
even the one winking of Paganini,
flew in and out of f-holes—

Wanting Sumptuous Havens

after Robert Bly

Someone's grumbling among the scallops
and the clam's mouth is being kept shut. He
and She, shouldering their repose demigods,
want Hell to be and God to sun again.
Is there no end to this Rumpelstiltskin?
They want straw gold and a sleeping beauty.
But an auk on one leg in a clear fog,
kills its krill, and never seems discontent.

In a manner of speaking—
I'm not Your boob or hang-up.
I'm not feet first or a mangled machination.
Even when You left me to my dad
who belted the fronts and backs of my hands
for dimes, nickels, and pennies
I never stole from my brother,
I am still not Your work.

Letting Go Seeds

i.

These hands are mad eaters
splintering curtains into rowed
closures into gouged evenings
and torn is in bookends.

ii.

These hands want to squeeze
beyond the bite of frowning
between these feathers as puppet
quivers between these teeth
not found between lips
but in your neck toss
you, blank bulb.

iii.

As your hands split on me,
my hands wish for you
where it all started—
from the hard-cased pit.

iv.

These hands
trying to mule
on up to God
choose not to be
my last words,
I hunger for—

v.

instead, may our hands
scratch at our own heads
like we are cats with mange
kept all within the "family."

vi.

No one ever
warned me
about this state
of overly warmed
tempers—
and how guilt buds
on dislike

vii.

as you art forward with
the likes of telling these hands
how I should not squeeze
beyond the bitten frown found
between these feathers as puppet
quivers between these teeth
not found in your neck toss

and No, I don't respect you

viii.

but like how
the Good Book
suggests,

O placebo, here we go
downhill the ego

ix.

I know
it would be
better to
let it go
and let it be
but these hands
want to
let the whole
damn thing
gong

Even when I work to imagine thoughts to push You
into layers: Skin, Stalk, Seed, and Spirit—then translated again
like into an offspring, fists revving its voice
for a defining moment of freedom,
I'm still not Your work.

***

Even when You and you point to plot holes here;
a hole is a hole is a hole.

What We Wanted

he said several times my issues
are unsolicited, and any more clear-
cut confessions will prevent
his furthering self-disclosures.

he asked, if I'm such an 'expert'
at rhetoric, have I worked enough
at rethinking the meaning
of traumas and solicitations?

I and Thou and We

for Anne

Let us meet again
after church, we can be
each other's blank start,
a collection of stares
like two pennies found
stained from our voyages.
We can, each other shine,
turn in our pens, grab brooms,
sweep the chimney, square joints,
and water the flowers' dark bark.
We can make up stories
if we want
swapping tissue and saliva
until the corners of our
mouths burn. Let us
cough up smoke and liver.
Let us cough up
myrrh and Frankenstein.
Let us go back
to our crash and urn,
be a shadow puppet on the wall,
dear peahen, tearing butterfly.
We can sing and sigh
a bearded prize; we can chant
a small *fateri, profiteri*;
we can speak monologues,
drama, poems, and dialogues:

whatever you want
to confess
  and/or contest.

I am not Your work
even after swallowing
another handful of Bach flowers,
felt to be useless beta blockers
for performative acts
except
when dreaming
about eulogies and constitutions.

Hernia

She's tired of the protrusions,
the rouser stare, the probative mutter
of words. She's tired of the cold, hate
the hazard hint hazardous thin glance
sliding pass the bartender. She's tired
of the 'save me' stripping away the savory
celibate left at the brink of a barstool
as if charity because she looks spent, over-
drawn, rigid and heaped like a torn muscle.
I know the words, she tried, can be translatable,
but recognize whenever she drives that dark road
home, the tired self slipknots a song for her self
to sleep: a small elegy embraced in a small mutiny.

At the Wedding

and after ten years, my father
asked me how I am.
I think I only said
I was lactose intolerant
all those years he thought
I was troubled—
I wanted to say
I'm fine—I feel
as any dead body would feel
decorated before a procession.
I wanted to say
I wanted a thin slice,
but I think my mom
forced my hand down,
and from the cake knife—
I wanted to say
I'm fine—I'm good—
I'm fine—I didn't want
to say that every time
I see the glint of balloons
mapped out on occasions,
like people's heads bobbled
across a lawn like a dark forest
viewed from my childhood's
two-story home, an ambulance
sirens the blacktop driveway
for a blurred vision of father,
once tall like how I imagine
the tree of Good and Evil—on fire

Even if You had these humans
place the blame onto me
for being sexually attacked
in the backseat of a school bus
because I had fallen asleep—

even if my calling out to You
seemed more like a default than a scream
or the otherwise sound of distortion
or the bargaining of sound saturation,
or like frequencies, and a bit—
forgotten.

I'm still not Your work.

Identification

After being attacked:
to give up this search
to give up 100 meters,
once again,
he'll get the inner lane.
to give up my name
which means like God,
Maker of things unseen
proves it's not
like the greatest thing
and I am not a god—
a little like this harvester routine,
or this beatnik tantrum,
after tantrum, where I don't
want to forget what we were
when it's time for matters
of the brain studied on a tray,
or seen from dental decay
or like a four-handed duet folded
into an embalming fluid—
to give up
it's almost like the moment of being silenced
like the last thought of hands driving in
after the last of the Schubert thirds—

Intercession

Most nights you are the last face I see
as I pray with your picture in my hand
as if I had placed stone on you myself.

Most nights when I stare at your picture
in the way a little child stares at the rub
of dirty hands watered into cleanliness,
I wonder about the wilderness.

Sometimes I wonder why my parents
layered me with your saintly name.
Sometimes I wonder if my black hair
creeps down like a veil and coif.

Although we can't speak about it,
I feel we were adjusted, Catholic servants,
opening in our mouths from a hunger,
fathoming Our Father under Psalm 139:
for there is no hurt that is so deep
that God is not deeper—

This makes me think of us
together, staring down
at the dozens of carpenter ants,
in their small infinity-shaped bodies,
rummaging the glue and the candy,

while destroying the wooden corners
of my writing desk drawers.

This makes me feel uneasy.

Please, remind me again;
what should we do about them?

III.

In the Afterlight of Children

In the Afterlight

for Jordan and Liam

What is the speed of dark—
     sounds like what is the speed of black—
          or the speed of a stallion beauty turning corners—
What about wild horses barreling down a Moroccan beach?
What about a boy not foreign to me who sleeps in their path?
     What is the speed of dilations?
          or the speed of nervous systems?
      or the involuntary? the hard-wiring?
    and on the fritz?
What is the speed of forcible suspension?
      or the permanency of no return?
What is the speed of saying no? and meaning no more?
      Is it like the speed of being chased down?
        or the speed of light? or the sly
  of a streaming bullet?
Is it like the speed of ripping through cells?
    I wish I understood the physics,
      for it sounds like the speed of a bull
        ramming into a windowless matter—
      almost like the speed of a power outage?
   or powerless and under age—
for what *is* the speed of returning to a dark?
       or the closing and opening a wound?
        Is it like bagging a body?
     I wonder,
       what is the sound of the emergent spirit?
     Does it sing like a lark
   or spike like a nightingale?

The Goddamn Fire

for R

is gnawing at a charred frame and where the hell
were those beleaguers' water or the gods
after the in-timely rain dance? Where were these persons of fire
who can stint-quick with grace? The child is inside
harping on a window
like *unforsaken*—flashback scorched turn still turning,
but my childish skin did not move through any spectrums.
Not like the one housed in real heat
the one they called names at the bus stop
but that stopped because Margie's house stopped then Margie
stopped.
The color of butter-wash gone into flakes,
not even like a dough in an oven, forgotten.
Do you understand she *gone*
goddamnit

Meditation on Kevin Carter's Sudanese Child

In the photo's frame there appears:
a child, a vulture, and a desert.
The child is brown.
The vulture is brown.
The desert is also a brown.
The child's sex is unclear.
The vulture's sex is unclear.
The desert acts asexual.
The child is small like the vulture.
The vulture is big like the child.
The desert seems vast.
The child seems atypically bald.
The vulture's head is also bald.
The desert does not care what they wear.
The child's body is hunched like the vulture.
The vulture's body shadows the child.
The desert looks thirsty and hungry.
The child looks weak.
The vulture looks strong.
The desert seems weathered and unbothered.
The child looks asleep.
The vulture stalks the child.
The desert yawns from the heat.
The child is like a concentration camp.
The vulture is like the barbed wire.
The desert looks like a warring backdrop.
Sometimes a photographer
likes a backdrop to create a mood.

The vulture has an eye on the cameraman.
The cameraman has eyes on the child.
The child has no eyes we can see.
The cameraman knows patience.
The vulture also knows patience.
The child is impatient for its mother.
But the desert is known to make mirages.
The cameraman knows this is a food station.
The vulture knows this is a food station.
The child knows it's a feeding station.
The desert appears stationary.
The vulture also appears stationary.
The child appears stationary and dying.
The cameraman is stationary and dead.

Turned Away from 30 Hospitals in 2 Hours

I don't love her
but like a fly
I could not pass her by.

I wanted to kiss her hands
and ribbon the feet
with more than fog

rub time and olive oil
into wrinkles
overstretching into nest.

I wanted to toss her a white church
near to stream, and build a boat
timbered small to frame

and send her name off
as if she rolled from
a river who never grew so tired

to wake her,
but don't wake her—
no need wake her—

She is a dead world.

Barren formerly known as Cold Woman

You might as well put down a fire.
There is no water, no chirping frogs,
the snakes are at base mosaic.
There are no surprises here,
no branches blasting piñata shoots
and heavens no starry color candies.
She is empty.
I know that you want to look
down in between her legs,
but double over the edge
and there you will find no one.
Try to touch her and she becomes
the goose runner. The fugitive fish.
Inside those hips, she wants to lay
out the world according to Genesis,
but monarchs, please find
honeycomb elsewhere.
She's only filled the Word.
Her yelling tits have locked their doors,
no men wooden in her windows.
I am telling you no one lives there anymore,
don't you get it?

You can't move her.
She's been pew-high praying
by a dried river stumped

for a miracle for ten, twelve,
what thirty years, waiting
for this rain to come, and so far,
there's only been the sin.

Ain't No Sunshine

and got no wildflower face either
running in backstroke
somewhere on her blonder porch

but she ain't asking for no Lazarus
or staffing a flask after hours
with the mean *Jesus, please.*

Sure, she had some moaning,
but she didn't give up the boy
like holding snakes up for birds

and like some women
she ain't drowning in her fishing state.

She's strong. Staying in line
every day
flat as sand dollar honey bait

where there ain't no prick in that pond—
where there ain't no son.

Meditation on the Lynching Photograph

She was once nothing to see
　　　　but you see now, she's someone, a young mother
　　　　turning in her house, up in smoke—
where the *God's* folk first passed her into a theatrical wind
　　　　of munitions, where her stomach's grip was gutted
　　　　　　　　of her hemmed infant—
　　　　　　　　and I know in this case,
　　　　one might think she could not possibly be strung up
　　　　rawboned on a poplar tree,
but in this case, like many enclosed cases, she was too,
　　　　along with her four small children

Predator

This story barely to begin does not die yet—

Wait.

for the last appendage, a slow smoking

snake—

Wait—

for the sweating egress—

and

Later, in a lake, in a slake lake, the bluest X—

Meditation on Pollock's *Troubled Queen*

She slopes across a Peconic boat. She weeps. No girder. No gown, except for the body of he who bears her name. No name. She cannot sleep with the silence of what should have been a valerian earpiece. She cannot sleep even when I send her countless sheep to stream their shanks into the geodesy. Nothing to sound but slit bangles to slave off into black water. She holds well her wild off, for his body is blue-green, gray and Quiet as a boy who lost manhandling the night swamp Despite She as moon-woman Despite She who is birdess churning up air as She gets to wear the death of puccoons in her hair hoary and ornery with an ostrich eye She unhinges mushroom like the crude toss of a duvet bent between her legs Man onto woman Water on water Ice for ice See for the seed has dropped as fruit found to be wormed rotten, but we kiss her up to God, as she kissed him up to dead-blue arms of Kali. Pulse is a rain dance. Justice is a secret king in the wings. There is a Storm coming She waits fisted for and for the thrown sub rosa, yes, there is a storm she waits for, like a wolf monstering up, sheer red ballyhoo.

A Mirror of Meat

She was most mornings
a thumb-sucker, not admitting

she had an appetite-fracture.
When the pig-headed parent didn't notice,

she would bandana the soft-
boiled egg beneath the tablecloth.

By most evenings, she was again
learning how to labor in the mouth,

the vertebral meat and this
would blush he, as if she

was caught with a cavernous thief,
a fang-patsy, redeeming juice

seemingly from a urethra-sponge
or better yet, she like from most vomit-

addendum would bellow out
like an animal from spear-tearing down.

A Mirror of Pretty Fungus

Pretty Fungus likes to hide under the backyard deck.
However, she doesn't like her picture taken like the family cat.

Pretty Fungus does not like being chased and dragged
through the grass like a wheelbarrow.

Pretty Fungus does not like getting bit inside the bushes
where bugs are gambit and rather rampant.

Pretty Fungus when forced to unbutton down
feels like throwing up.

She's a real peach, but we all have two faces.

Pretty Fungus doesn't like to grow in her home.
She often likes running into the neighbor's doorbell.

Pretty Fungus doesn't know why it makes her cold,
but she knows something about cherry-flavored popsicles pooled overnight.

A Mirror of Defiance

She was a Temple of the Holy Ghost
who swore she didn't have a thing

but a piece of beef liver on her plate
and no real pleasure poking at it.

And said her grace? She hadn't
and today would be no different than none

except today's prayers
she had only tried to say three times

but she instead said right to the dog left aside:
help me not to be so mean

and yes,
he was looking up at her

with those lion eyes of paradise
his mouth left ajar for a poke

and yes, she felt
his cage of fire at her feet

as if she would do it
as if she would stomp him right out

Meditation on Yiadom-Boakye's *Nous Etions*

He eyeliners in the dark hours,
            a debutante, and he's got skills,
like a bird of reason, a beacon
            of the dressing-room, *the* omega black-moustache
among the woodworkers in this paradise
bare-bass quiet,
        machismo left as a distance stain
            as you get to know him little
       by little wino, and promise,
            he'll frame you up,
      Voyeur
he might call at a falcon slant,
        although he likes the attention
            and at a distance kept
          cheek to light blush to cheek
       like the north-side of the hillside,
         it's his best jaw line.
What do you think of me, Ms. Visine?
            Are we smudged yet?
Should we go for smoky broke?

A Prayer formerly known as Always

There is so much to say
like so many singing into their hymnals
yellow, like yellow a doctor would tell you
of jaundice walls, but we were saying
there are so many tongues who slingshot
so many words aired into concrete,
so many shapely fences
to kick on down and splint
while reaching into the cleavage.
My how we perk up those pez-dispensers,
and even when the color of my basmati
shines his name in my crock-pot, dearie,
there are so many like this hiding
behind the porn-shop door,
leaving their skin of maple dead in a frame.
Didn't we say there are so many dead,
singing we all are sinners?
We all are sinners.
We all are beggars
heaped into the corner
somewhat clothed on a cold road
that is truly praying something here.
I am truly praying something here,
my God, how I hate what the signs say—
my God, they say *this* is usage in vain.

Prayer

O Complacency
Here is wholly for you
childless and unbridled
I am your epilogue
and threadbare
Here is mistletoe Here
under music
under tongues
artful and litmus
undistinguished and seedy
descendant of descendant
ferocious parched and devout
is the heart of your heart
broken and drained as a fistula
for good measure
and I understand
I would shake my finger too
if I were criticizing you
parental and tyrannical
but I could never understand
why break from us then break us apart

Floaters

I have yet to learn, why hurricane the trees
      bending nests and necks down until they snap
         and migrate in all the wrong, wrong spaces
    like the boats un-strapping, one by one under the waters
like an unbeliever caught in a killer stare
      between lands and the wild fever for escape.
         Some nights, memory writhes in the spark,
    and even when striding fingers over ears, faint still screams,
         as a river does trying to keep a royal tone
    over rocks, and cars, and debris,
            but I cannot stop un-strapping the waters in replay
        while minding the push through these rural parts,
    but still, we nest in the aftermath of trees. If we could only fly,
mind to be that head, like a cockerel
    witnessing the twist of humans thinned
        almost as unruly kites,
         strung and fallen under the wrung, wrung parts—

The Old Bones

The oldest country of my bones act
        as stint and skin of independence
                perhaps like an introduction to intra and inter
        or the precursors of discovering indentures
like mule donkey carriage
        sturm und drang muscles und motor cars
                are all fads in the intestines
                        the old bones don't quite forget
                the two by two by two by twos
        or who took stock or who took whipcord
and who took plain horse power
        or pain as veined attempts
                wedded unwanted companionship and then reproduced
        like a master who becomes mired masters
the old bones quietly quilted myriads of skills
        texturing furrowed brows and tremors
        like the tapestry of testimonials
                these old bones grind their teeth in my sleep
                        utter words I cannot make out
                                for I can tell from the pined irises even
                                in the dead night
                blued browned solid and blacked
them old bones know I could not possibly know
        the moment before the back is forced to bend
                and the whole of a hand collars
                        like a remote leash on a mutt overly tense to a
                        sonic alert

how funny the bones are the almost invisible
as a thin line of an air draft
　　　　that crawls off almost every measured
　　　　　　and unmetered breath

Process

Sometimes I'm a well-carved straggler
                                inside this kid.
Sometimes I'm a beginner
                        rubbing my nicked billiard again.
Somewhere I am a life guard inside
                                downing on the observers,
        while sometimes I'm the halter falling
                                from shoulders and I switch
                                        panic for play.
        At some point I was swimming
                        in boys too big
                                between the high-five divers
            and pushed play under the panic
but you never quite had the water in the cry
                                'cause you burned in timeshares
        and kissed as a wet deposit does
                        chemicals on chemicals
            and for you I am only the next inhale
                        I am only a fern gully
of green sea and sometimes you are a mouthful of sand
                        and sometimes I am a good shot-put spitter
        but I will crawl forever to the edge of almost
                                just like you.
            And yes sometimes I am drowning in the saved
                and a stroke in the tide pulley.
Sometimes I am the sheet-surge,
                the pond, the ocean, the drool string, the coconut split.

I am a worm
and can't breathe.
The mourning dove
is playing with its form.
I am draining when I can't see you,
but you see me. And Yes
sometimes you do see me
stopped at the shoulders,
when the I am is folded down.
Someday I will no longer be for sale
just like barnacles
of one forgetful, after another, or perhaps just
missing in the garage,
and the blamer of tall-tell garbage
as you look for me and play kitchen gloves panic on your face
as I console the yes, here I am still
somewhere in the quilted damage
hushed in a mountain
dumpster green
where I will be resting
and Yes
I'll be resting with you.

Notes

"A Partial Cento of Visible Light" is a cento, citing the following poets, in the order in which their lines, or edited version, appear: / 4 Scott Hightower / 5 James Merrill / 6 Star Black / 7 Grace Schulman / 8 Matthea Harvey / 9 Anne Sexton / 11 Sharon Olds / 12 David Bergman / 13 Shara McCallum / 14 Derek Walcott / 16 Seamus Heaney / 18 Yusef Komunyakaa / 19 Edna St. Vincent Millay / 20 James Tate/ 21 Frederick Seidal / 22 Billy Collins/ 23 Bob Hicok / 24 Mankh / 25 Elizabeth Bishop / 26 Jill Bialosky / 27 Terrance Hayes / 28 Anne Sexton / 30 Robert Creeley

"A Bishop in the Sky" is inspired by Elizabeth Bishop's poem "Little Exercise."

"After the Emergency" is based on Matthea Harvey's poem "Set Your Sights."

In "Warning Report," some words were taken from a local Long Island weather report in Sept 2016.

"Wanting Sumptuous Havens" is based on Robert Bly's poem "Wanting Sumptuous Heavens."

"At the Wedding" uses inspired lines *Balloons on the mailbox, ambulance in the driveway* from Amit Majmudar's poem "By Accident."

"Meditation on Pollock's Troubled Queen" is inspired by Jackson Pollock's painting "Troubled Queen."

"A Mirror of I and Thou and We" is in dialogue with Anne Sexton's poem "The Fury of Sundays."

"A Mirror of Defiance" is inspired by Flannery O'Conner's short story, "The Temple of the Holy Ghost."

"Meditation on Yiadom-Boakye's Nous Etions" was commission by Cave Canem for Yiadom-Boakye's exhibit at The Studio Museum in Harlem, NYC.

Acknowledgments

Deepest thanks and internal acclamations to the following journals, publications, readers, and editors who first published (and reprinted) the following poems, or earlier versions, found in this collection:

Cave Canem Anthology XIII: "Blank Canvas"
Drunken Boat: "The Goddamn Fire"
Grabbing the Apple: "Predator"
great weather for MEDIA: "Hunt"
Lemon Hound: "The Floater" ("Floaters")
Long Island Sounds: "Five Transient Months"
Long Island Quarterly: "Zen Press to Ithaca"
New Yorker: "Process"
Narrative Magazine: "A Mirror of a Mirror"
Paumanok, Interwoven: "A Bishop in the Sky" and "Dear Tornado" ("Flat Winds also known as Tornado")
Southampton Review: "After Dinner," "Stones formerly known as Love," "Barren formerly known as Cold Woman," "Lynching the Mrs." ("Meditation on the Lynching Photograph"), "Ain't No Sunshine," "Turned Away After 30 Hospitals in 2 Hours," "A Prayer formerly known as Always," "A Mirror of Pretty Fungus," "A Mirror of Meat," and "The Engagement Ring"
Transition Magazine: "Meditation on Kevin Carter's Sudanese Child" and "The Old Bones"
Xanadu: "Butterfly" ("A Mirror of the Black Swallowtail")
Vinyl Poetry: "Meditation on Pollock's *Troubled Queen*"
White Space Anthology: "Stones formerly known as Love" and "The Floater" ("Floaters")

Thank you to Stony Brook University-Southampton MFA, Southampton Writers' Conference, Cave Canem Foundation/workshops, Bread Loaf Writers' Conference/workshops, Walt Whitman Birthplace, and the Long Island poetry community.

Special thanks to Julie Sheehan, Star Black, Terrance Hayes, Bob Reeves, Tara Propper Kelly, Tara Kavanagh, Shirine Babb, Carrie Addington, Maya Washington, LB Thompson, Thomas Lux, Andrea Horn, Lou Ann Walker, George Dorsty, Gene Hammond, Kristina Lucenko, Charif Shanahan, Kathy Donnelly, Brigit Buhle, June Whittaker, Jane Ormerod and Editors at great weather for MEDIA.

Many thanks to those whose teaching, advice and/or support aided the evolution of poems in this manuscript: Derek Walcott, Cornelius Eady, Yusef Komunyakaa, Toi Derricotte, Roger Rosenblatt, Carl Phillips, Billy Collins, Jean Valentine, Paul Muldoon, Linda Gregerson, Ama Codjoe, George Wallace, Will and Annette Chandler, Matthew Kremer, Kelly Powell, Russ Green, Liam Murphy, Benjamin Goldberg, Amisha Patel, Matthew Miranda, Spencer Sutherland, Melissa Fadul, Shara McCallum, Kristina Lucenko, Rashmi Rai, MaryAnn Duffy, Kempton van Hoff, Tammy Nuzzo-Morgan, Lucas Hunt, Alan Semerdjian, Otar, Sue and Mike Yankowski, Pat Secko, Donald Bohlen, Christopher Byrd, Adrienne Unger, Tula Holmes, Brian Whittaker, Marie Oliver, Audrey Robinson, Marilyn Vogel and II.

About the Author

Michelle Whittaker is a poet and musician. Her poems have been published in *The New Yorker*, *Southampton Review*, *Narrative*, *Vinyl*, *Transitions Magazine*, *Long Island Quarterly*, and other publications. She was awarded a Jody Donohue Poetry Prize and Cave Canem Fellowship. She is an Assistant Professor in the Program of Writing and Rhetoric at Stony Brook University.

About great weather for MEDIA

Founded in January 2012, great weather for MEDIA focuses on the unpredictable, the fearless, the bright, the dark, and the innovative…

We are based in New York City and showcase both national and international writers. As well as publishing the highest quality poetry and prose, we organize numerous readings, performances, music and art events in New York City, across the United States, and beyond.

Be sure to visit our website for details of upcoming publications, events, weekly open mic, and how to submit work to great weather for MEDIA's yearly anthology.

Website: www.greatweatherformedia.com

Email: editors@greatweatherformedia.com

Twitter: @greatweatherfor

Facebook: www.facebook.com/great.weather

Instagram: greatweatherformedia

www.greatweatherformedia.com

great weather for MEDIA Titles

Collections

Surge - Michelle Whittaker

Crown Prince of Rabbits - John Paul Davis

Exercises in High Treason - John J. Trause

Harvest the Dirt - Wil Gibson

Debridement - Corrina Bain

meant to wake up feeling - Aimee Herman

Retrograde - Puma Perl

Anthologies

The Other Side of Violet

The Careless Embrace of the Boneshaker

Before Passing

I Let Go of the Stars in My Hand

The Understanding between Foxes and Light

It's Animal but Merciful